Remembering Chris

Also by Rosalie Calabrese

Writer's Choice
New York, NY: Katydid Press, 2000

In Print
New York, NY: Katydid Press, 2002

Growing Up Jewish
New York, NY: Katydid Press, 2005

A Few Poems for Hard Times
New York, NY: Katydid Press, 2009

Zine workers
with Mark Sonnenfeld
East Windsor, NJ: Marymark Press, 2010

Remembering Chris

Poems by

Rosalie Calabrese

POETS WEAR PRADA • Hoboken, New Jersey

Remembering Chris

Copyright © 2015 Rosalie Calabrese

Poets Wear Prada
533 Bloomfield Street, Second Floor
Hoboken, New Jersey 07030
http://pwpbooks.blogspot.com

First North American Publication 2015.
First Mass Market Paperback Edition 2015.

Grateful acknowledgment is made to the following publications where some of these poems have appeared or are forthcoming:

And Then; *Mom Egg Review*; *Nomad's Choir*; *Jewish Women's Literary Annual*; *Möbius, The Poetry Magazine*; *Psychoanalytic Perspectives*; *Thirteen Poetry Magazine*; and *Messages from Mothers to Sons* (Pittsfield, NH: Lynxfield Publishing, 2003).

ISBN-13: 978-0692303795
ISBN-10: 0692303790

Printed in the U.S.A.

Front Cover Image: Calabrese Family Archives
Author Photo: Bonnie Geller-Geld

In memoriam,
Christopher Jordan Calabrese
(1966 – 2007)

Table of Contents

Remembering
Chris

Mixed Emotions

October 11, 1966

Newly graduated from the Red Cross
diaper-folding class,
Lamaze the buzzword,
I opt for sodium pentothal
and a good sleep,
leaving my mother to count toes,
check weight, hold your first bottle,
make sure the scrotum's intact.
A scrawny 22 inches,
you know better than to cry
when she hands you over
cleverly binding me with lashes
already long as your father's,
eyes the color of an Italian plum.

Thorns

Fresh from the schoolyard
my son eagerly shows off
the latest addition to his vocabulary,
a word he can only define
by an obscene gesture.
I take a queenly stance,
say, "We are not amused";
yet he pricks me with the thorn again.
Sorely tried, I change my tactic,
insist he repeat the offense
a hundred times more.
He stops at eighty — enough for a lifetime.
Though temporarily relieved,
I dread what's left unsaid.

Parents' Day

Convinced you're having fun at camp,
We start to drive away,
But then we see you hiding in the car
Like a fugitive on the lam.

While we take you back
To finish out your sentence,
We wonder if you'll ever forgive us
For loving you so much.

New Year's Eve, Mexico City

It really isn't safe to wander after sundown,
though half the post-siesta fun is finding
dark addresses where chefs earn guidebook stars.
Tonight in Zona Rosa without a reservation,
the divorce decree I've carried from New York
still inside my purse, I let my teenage son
lead me through the shadows beyond
the crowded restaurants, my spirits
falling faster than the ball in Times Square,
while I consider the merits of tacos to go.

At last, an open door. Balloons and candles
promise to restore my festive mood.
Not a spot for locals, this place
is more a gathering of tribes.
Passports at the hat check, we're greeted
in language approximating English.
The menu, too, invokes a taste of home —
sauces on the side. Midnight,
the waiters chime, "*¡Champán!*"

Then, "*¡Bailar!*" A mariachi band appears. My son,
to everyone's delight, dances with a chair.
Babble, bubbles, fiesta in my brain,
I make divorce confetti and fling it in the air.
Hugs and kisses all around,
we say farewell as if we'll meet again,
share balloons and candlelight;
the streets of Mexico City, safe at night.

At Christmas

"Belén, campanas de Belén,"
I practiced all through Chanukah,
in the soprano section
of my high school Spanish chorus.

Ecumenical ahead of the pope,
my family put up a Christmas tree
that even rivaled Mrs. O'Connell's
in the apartment next door.

She and her sister the nun
applauded while my brother
ran his Lionels over the fake snow
so fast they crashed into each other —
like dissenting religions.

Tonight on a train that's careening
toward this mostly Spanish neighborhood
where taxi drivers warn me
to keep my doors locked,
I hear a woman say, "You should go to Israel;
it's cheap once you get there."

Her Yiddish lilt makes me think
how I named my son Christopher
without paying attention to the meaning,
before I became an alto
and forgot the rest of the song.

A Memo to My Son

You had no bris,
And you had no bar-mitzvah,
But make no mistake, my son:
You are the flesh of my flesh,
And the blood of my blood;
When all the scores are tallied,
You will still be a Jew.

As I Passed By ...

   the toddler in a pink sweater said,
very clearly, to the man who held her hand,
"I want to go home."
Her grandfather — I think it was —
smoothed her hair and said, "Soon,
in another week or so. It'll be all right."

Her sobs followed me around
the corner into a memory
where my son never forgave me
for leaving him with relatives
when I took my first trip to Europe,
a direct flight from the hub of divorce.

When her parents return,
will they talk of battling an illness, or
of dancing away on a second honeymoon?
And when the girl grows up,
will the woman in the pink sweater
need to leave her child behind,
while she goes off to live her life —
maybe to save it
in another week or so?

On Your Wedding Day

In the refrigerator
Bottles of my nail polish
Stand in place of baby formula;
In your room
Only a tuxedo hangs in the closet
Which through the years
Housed your toys in scrambled disarray;
When that suit is gone
I'll move my clothes
Into the empty space
And sleep in the bed
Where boyhood dreams
Are held for safekeeping.

At Our Son's Wedding

Side by side at our son's wedding
Unable to believe how time has flown
Or how far you and I have grown apart
We remember when love was a song
Played on a small boy's heartstrings
And share a silent prayer
That his promises will keep.

In Your New Home

For My Daughter-in-Law

This rocking chair,
where once I held my son
and sang a mother's lullabies,
I now pass along to you.
As we three join together
in a toast, I wish you all the joy
this chair has brought to me.

Pregnant

Those last three months
of pickles dripping brine
and aromatic spices
fresh from the barrel,
potatoes fried to a golden turn
in the fish market's bubbling oil,
ice cream covered with walnuts
and frozen chocolate sauce,
I watched your father put on weight.
Now, as your wife feeds her cravings,
and it's you who's growing baby fat,
I'm swelling up with joy.

To My Son at Thirty

It's odd that you've turned thirty
and I'm still "thirty-nine."
Had I held out for a leap year,
you'd now be seven and a half.

If you keep having birthdays
while I stay where I am,
someday I'll surely hear you saying,
"You're just too young to understand."

Tropical Storm Chris

Huddled onshore while the waves churn
as if coming and going at the same time
I remember how my own stormy Chris
broke water breached against the tide
and how resistance to the natural flow of things
can cause more turbulence than one might expect.

For My Son
On Father's Day, 1998

With osteoporosis throwing me a curve,
I shift into reverse
on the road that brought us here today.
At the miniature village you made
when model railroads were your passion,
I stop to remember:
how you laid the track and nailed it down,
gathered your own steam to huff and puff
past each closed-off station;
while I ran the shuttle
between career and motherhood.
So often, our line of communication
filled with static — almost disconnected;
I feared you'd lose your way.
But, as you bend to embrace me now,
wife and daughter by your side,
despite my diminished height,
I feel tall.

Stirring the Pot

My husband called me "mouse,"
a term of endearment
I should have questioned
from the start.
My father's "princess,"
though more pleasing,
is questionable as well.
Both of them
led me down the aisle —
Adam, on the sidelines,
calling his wife, Eve,
"my little apple."
Now I hear my son
call his daughter "little noodle"
and suspect he doesn't know
what he's really cooking.

Money for Your Birthday

The year your father gave me
tires for the car I never drove,
I fell into despair but still
I kept on buying him
the clothes he'd never wear.
These days I've tried to mend my ways,
so you'll find a check inside this box
and oh, what the heck — a pair of sox.

On Shavu'ot

My grandchild asks what Jewish people believe in.
Her parents giving me that wide-eyed look that signals,
"Help!" I jump in and bumble my way through
Sunday School platitudes: love, kindness, respect, etc.
Each one elicits a jaded silence from the kid.

I suspect I'm losing ground but can only think of
Pain, prejudice, persecution —
Not what I want to tell a five-year-old who still finds
Scary moments in *Winnie-the-Pooh.*
"C'mon," she says, "like in the scroll, the Torah."
Now that I've led her to the place where my roots
Lie tangled within a borrowed name,
Can I confess I don't remember,
Maybe never even knew? Undone,
I tell my son to look for an answer on the Web.

A Mother's Lament

Here, now, a chance to tell you
the measure of my love,
describe the gardens of my heart
where you are every flower,
but all I do is ask how things are going,
as if we'd met just recently
at a crowded party,
and it's only your smile that I recall.

Thinking of Chris

I. On a Quiet Morning, 2000

The silence envelops me the way it did
When you first went off to college,
And we made a break
It took all four years to mend;
Not able to say then
What was really on my mind
Haunts me now like the ghost
Of your father seeking closure.
In some future time,
If I come back to bother you
With unfinished business,
Hold this paper to the light;
It will serve as proof
That some mistakes are unerasable.

II. Remembering, 2008

Always with me now ...
Not in body ... the last image of you
Lying in that box like a stuffed doll,
Muscle and bone discharged to science ...
Only the times of joy and sorrow
Still alive, each demanding equal attention ...
Partying in Mexico City on New Year's Eve
Pitted against the waiting for your father
Those Sundays when he didn't show up ...
Your anger taken out on me as a last resort
To hold on to your sanity...
Finally bringing me to my knees
As I apologize for every pain you ever felt,
Never to know if I am forgiven.

Prayers for Hope and Comfort

So many times, yearning for hope and comfort,
yet closed off to them by my own resolve to stay strong:
I've left a gift from a well-meaning friend —
this book of prayers — unopened; but yesterday,
the pileup of grief grown too large,
I placed this offering of hope and comfort
in a space of its own, on the desk,
apart from the accumulation of other,
possibly never-to-be-read, books,
and there it sits like a trophy for an iron will.

Lachrymal

Not gathered into glass vials
below ground as in ancient Rome,
tears like mine for a child outlived
lie deep within a stony sigh
until a glancing remark
finds the fault line.

Beyond Night

Your shadow lingers
like the scent of mint
on summer's breath,
enticing me to follow.
In the bleak hours,
I reach for your hand
and hold the memory.

"Tear Here for Easy Separation"

A little in the heart, a little in the gut,
a head too thick to tear with bare emotions,
one would think I'd have let you go by now,
an easy separation of rendered parts
that once made up a whole.
No, not so fast, not yet,
if ever ...

Forever

Your smile in the photo above my desk
prompts me to fill my calendar
even when I wonder why I should
or wish I could believe
we'll meet again in heaven.
Women long ago simply
threw themselves into the burial pit,
but they were the wives,
and I am only the mother,
the one who takes the proverbial hit
and turns it into a lifelong *kvetch*,
a gag that keeps me smiling,
forever, back at you.

Acknowledgments

We extend our thanks to the following publications where some of these poems first appeared or are forthcoming:

And Then	"A Memo to My Son," "At Our Son's Wedding," "Thinking of Chris"
Mom Egg Review (formerly known as *The Mom Egg*)	"Pregnant," "A Mother's Lament," "On Shavu'ot"
Nomad's Choir	"Thorns"
Jewish Women's Literary Annual	"Beyond Night"
Möbius, The Poetry Magazine	"New Year's Eve, Mexico City"
Psychoanalytic Perspectives	"Mixed Emotions"
Thirteen Poetry Magazine	"On Your Wedding Day"
Messages from Mothers to Sons, compiled by Mary E. Brown. Pittsfield, NH: Lynxfield Publishing, 2003.	"To My Son at Thirty," "For My Son on Fathers Day, 1998"

"New Year's Eve, Mexico City" was one of twelve poems selected by *Möbius, The Poetry Magazine* for its 2011 Editor-in-Chief's Choice Awards.

About the Author

Rosalie Calabrese is a native New Yorker who works as a management consultant for the arts. Her publication credits include *Cosmopolitan*, *Poetry New Zealand*, *Poetica*, *Jewish Currents*, *Mom Egg Review*, and *The New York Times*. Her poems have frequently been set to music as art songs by various composers including Eugene McBride and Leonard Lehrman. She has also collaborated with several composers writing the lyrics and libretti for musicals; among them — *Friends and Relations* and *Not in Earnest* (both with composer Anthony Calabrese) and *Moving On* (music by Blair Weille). Her musicals have been performed in New York, Vermont, and California.

For over thirty years she served as Executive Director for the American Composers Alliance, representing three hundred composers of concert music, a roster including Francis Thorne and Richard Danielpour. Her private clients have included the pianist Margaret Mills, photographer Margaret McCarthy, singer-songwriter Peggy Seeger, and the composers Arthur Berger and Irving Fine, among others.

Remembering Chris is her sixth book of poetry.

A NOTE ON THE TYPE

This book is set in Gentium Book Basic, a typeface designed by J. Victor Gaultney and released with Gentium Basic in 2007 (test version) and in 2008 (final version). The Gentium family of typefaces was first conceived by Gaultney in 2000 to fulfill part of the requirements for the Master of Arts in Typeface Design at the University of Reading, United Kingdom. Gaultney's Gentium combines the aesthetics of its calligraphic foundation with best-in-practice modern day typography design to provide an attractive and legible type.

Gentium was publicly released in 2002 and received a Certificate of Excellence in Type Design in 2003 as part of the Bukva:raz! (or "Letter:One!") type design competition sponsored by the Association Typographique Internationale (ATypI). In this international design competition where 251 designers from 30 countries participated, and over 600 entries competed, Gentium was honored as one of the best designs of the past five years.

Gentium Book Basic is a slightly heavier variation of its partner font, Gentium Basic, which make it an ideal choice for print publications. The 'Basic' fonts only support a limited Latin character set (no Greek or Cyrillic). Gaultney has since developed Gentium Plus, an extension to the original 'Basic' character set, which includes extended Latin glyphs (Unicode 7.0), archaic Greek symbols, and full extended Cyrillic script support. The Gentium Plus font family currently includes only regular and italic faces.

The Gentium font families are freely available and may be used by anyone at no cost. They were first released under the SIL Open Font License, a free and open source license that permits modification and redistribution, in September of 2003.